BLUEPRINTS BEAT COCKTAIL NAPKINS

HOW TO CREATE A WINNING BUSINESS PLAN FOR GROWTH AND PROFIT

BRIDGET McCREA

STRONGTIDE PRESS

Copyright ©2025 by StrongTide Press. All rights reserved. No part of this book may be reproduced, stored in a retrieval system or transmitted in any form or by any means without the prior written consent of the publisher, except in the case of short quotations used in reviews, blogs or articles.

ISBN 978-0-9970454-7-5 (paperback)
ISBN 978-0-9970454-8-2 (ebook)

First Edition

Published by StrongTide Press

www.strongtidepress.com

Printed and distributed in the United States of America

This book is for informational and educational purposes only. The author is not an attorney, accountant or financial advisor and the book is not meant to provide legal, tax or financial advice. Laws, rules and requirements change and every business situation is different, so please consult a qualified professional for guidance specific to you.

Any products, services, URLs or organizations mentioned are included for reference only. The author has no affiliation, endorsement or agreements with them. Use your own judgment before acting on any information provided in the following pages.

Contents

INTRODUCTION: YOUR LAUNCHPAD TO PROFIT 1
Show the World (and Yourself) that You've Thought this Through 3
Who is This Book For? 5
Before We Dive In 7
4 Ways to Crush Your Business Planning Game 8

CHAPTER 1: MAP OUT YOUR MONEY JOURNEY FIRST 9
Don't Go Broke Before You Go Big 10
It's Time for a Financial Gut Check 11
The Financial Realities of Business Ownership 14
Let's Put Your Financial Data to Work 17
4 Quick Money Preservation Tips 19

CHAPTER 2: STACK THE DECK IN YOUR FAVOR 21
It's a Plan, Not the Great American Novel 23
4 Planning Hacks That Actually Work 26

CHAPTER 3: YOUR INTERACTIVE BUSINESS PLAN WORKBOOK 27
Beyond the Basics: Optional Sections That Add Value 42
A Map for Handling the Twists, Turns and Roadblocks 43
4 Ways to Gain a Planning Edge 45

CHAPTER 4: SERVICE BUSINESS PLAN BLUEPRINT 47

CHAPTER 5: BUILD YOUR PRODUCT PLAN 59

CHAPTER 6: DON'T FILE YOUR PLAN AWAY. ACTIVATE IT! 71
Your Annual Growth Check-In 73
Your Success Journey Starts Here 74
Four Winning Ways to Maximize Your 75
Planning Investment 75

CHAPTER 7: 10 BONUS TIPS FOR BUSINESS PLANNING SUCCESS 77
Your Next Steps Start Now 80

Startup Resource Hub 83
Recap: All Your Power Tips in One Place 93

References 97
About the Author 99
Unlock Your Exclusive Business Planning Toolkit 101
Share Your Experience & Help Others Start Smart 103

INTRODUCTION: YOUR LAUNCHPAD TO PROFIT

"A good business plan guides you through each stage of starting and managing your business. You'll use your business plan as a roadmap for how to structure, run and grow your new business. It's a way to think through the key elements of your business." --U.S. Small Business Administration

Getting into something without first laying out a plan is pretty darned human, right? We love to jump into new things, explore the opportunities, get our feet wet and just "see how things go." Sometimes this Curious George-esque mindset gets you into trouble and other times everything just works out fine. Most times we land somewhere in the middle: maybe not thrilled with the end results but no biggie; we'll live to see another day (and, do it all over again).

Business ownership doesn't have to be such a crapshoot. In fact, it shouldn't be. The numbers don't lie: many new businesses fail within their first few years. Not because the owners weren't smart or hardworking, but because they skipped the boring stuff (like figuring out if anyone actually wants what they're selling or whether they can make money doing it).

You wouldn't renovate your kitchen without measuring the space first, but many people start businesses without knowing their <u>basic costs</u>. They dive in headfirst, then act surprised when the money runs out faster than expected. It's like driving cross-country without first checking to make sure your car can make the trip.

The good news is that a business plan isn't some academic exercise designed to torture aspiring entrepreneurs. It's a tool for figuring out whether your great idea can actually work in the real world. It forces you to do the math, identify potential problems and come up with solutions before you're frantically Googling "how to save my failing business" while stress-eating cereal at 2AM.

So what does the planning process actually look like? I'm not going to sugarcoat it; it's not very glamorous. You'll spend time researching competitors, crunching numbers and asking yourself uncomfortable questions about your assumptions. But here's the payoff: when you're done, you'll have something most entrepreneurs never get. Genuine confidence that your business can and will succeed.

Show the World (and Yourself) that You've Thought this Through

Uncle Sam (or more specifically, the U.S. Small Business Administration) defines a good business plan as a <u>roadmap that guides you through each stage of starting and managing your business</u>. "Business plans can help you get funding or bring on new business partners," it says.

"Investors want to feel confident they'll see a return on their investment. Your business plan is the tool you'll use to convince people that working with you — or investing in your company — is a smart choice."

According to Investopedia, the best business plans outline a company's objectives and strategies and that they're a key ingredient for startups that want to attract potential investors, lenders and partners. And NerdWallet says that a well-written business plan should hit on all of the important points related to your company's goals, products, services and finances.

As you can see, everyone has their own way of describing what a business plan should do, but they're all dancing around the same basic idea. The plan is your chance to prove you've thought this through. Call it a roadmap, a strategy outline or a tool for convincing investors, it all boils down to one thing: you're showing the world (and yourself) that you understand what you're getting into and have a reasonable plan for making it work.

Done right, your plan will also help you obtain funding, bring on new business partners and simply keep your underlying "plan of action" on track by getting your best ideas out of your head and onto paper or the computer screen, whatever works best for your particular brand of organized chaos.

15 Reasons NOT to Write a Business Plan

Before we dive into creating your business plan, let's address a reality that you all knew was coming: most people avoid writing business plans like they avoid going to the dentist. They know it's probably good for them, but they'd rather do almost anything else. Here are some common excuses for skipping the planning stage and jumping in with both feet:

1. I don't have time to write a business plan. I'm too busy trying to get this thing started.
2. Business plans are for corporate types, not scrappy entrepreneurs like me.
3. My idea is so obviously good that detailed planning would just slow me down.
4. I started writing one but got overwhelmed by all the sections and requirements.
5. Business plans are boring, and I'd rather focus on the exciting stuff.
6. I don't want to overthink it and kill my enthusiasm for the project.

7. Plans are too rigid, and I need flexibility to pivot when opportunities arise.
8. I don't know how to do financial projections and the numbers intimidate me.
9. What if I write it all down and discover my idea won't actually work?
10. Real entrepreneurs just figure it out as they go. Planning is for people who lack confidence.
11. I'm waiting until I have more experience and knowledge before I start planning.
12. Business plans are just busy work that investors require. I'm bootstrapping this myself.
13. I tried using a template but it didn't fit my unique business model.
14. My industry moves too fast for traditional planning methods.
15. I'll create a plan once I get some traction and see where the business is headed.

Look, I get it. Any or all of these excuses feel justified when you're sitting there staring at a blank page. But here's the thing: you're going to invest months or years of your life into this venture. Isn't it worth spending a weekend figuring out if you're headed in the right direction? Your future self will thank you for doing the work now instead of scrambling to fix problems later.

Who is This Book For?

This book was designed for anyone who is ready to get serious about business planning, including:

- ➤ **Aspiring entrepreneurs** with a solid business concept who aren't sure how to turn their idea into a legitimate, operational company. This book provides the step-by-step guidance you've been missing.
- ➤ **Anyone overwhelmed by the startup process** who feels daunted by the sheer volume of information and tasks involved in launching a business. I'll break it down into manageable, actionable steps for you.
- ➤ **New and existing business owners** seeking a solid foundation. Whether you already have a company or are just starting out, if you don't have a business plan yet, you've come to the right place.
- ➤ **People ready to stop dreaming and <u>start doing</u>**. If you've been contemplating starting a business for a while and you're finally ready to take action, this book offers the practical tools and knowledge you need to move forward.

Maybe you fall into a different category and that's perfectly fine. I'll teach you how to build a robust business plan, get a realistic baseline on your current financial status and activate your plan in a way that works for your specific business. This book includes a complete workbook and two full sample plans (one for service businesses, one for product businesses), all of which are also available as digital downloads for free. You'll find the URLs for these resources at the end of the book on page 95.

Before We Dive In

I'm not a lawyer or a CPA and nothing in these pages should be mistaken for legal or tax advice. What you'll find here is for informational purposes only to help you get smarter about starting and running a business. Also, if I mention a product, website or organization, it's just an example. I don't have any fancy sponsorships, secret deals or backroom agreements with them. Think of it as me pointing out tools on the shelf, not handing out endorsements.

Whether you're in the early stages of starting a business or you've already started transacting business, this book is for you. I'm here to help you with all of the blocking and tackling involved with creating a success roadmap for your new or existing company. Everything you need to get started is in your hands: turn the page and let's start building your business success story today.

 **MAKE THIS YOUR NEXT STEP**

Kick off your plan by writing your business idea in one clear sentence.

4 Ways to Crush Your Business Planning Game

- ☑ **Do the boring stuff first.** Figure out if anyone actually wants what you're selling and whether you can make money doing it before you dive in headfirst.

- ☑ **Use your plan as proof you've thought this through.** Show the world (and yourself) that you understand what you're getting into and have a reasonable plan for making it work.

- ☑ **Don't let excuses derail your planning.** You're going to invest months or years into this venture, so it's worth spending a weekend figuring out if you're headed in the right direction.

- ☑ **Get your ideas out of your head and onto paper.** Transform your organized chaos into a concrete roadmap that keeps your plan of action on track.

1

MAP OUT YOUR MONEY JOURNEY FIRST

The national economy literally <u>runs</u> on entrepreneurial energy, with roughly 5 million new businesses launched every year. Small businesses make up 99.9% of all firms, employ nearly half of the nation's private sector workforce and account for more than 62% of net jobs created since 1995. On average, just over five million new businesses open in the U.S. every year.

Here's an eye-opener: only 33% of small businesses have a formal business plan in place. So most entrepreneurs navigate the complex business world without a clear roadmap, essentially hoping to build their futures by chance. Now consider this: 71% of fast-growing companies reportedly <u>use business plans</u>.

What's the lesson here? It's that passion and hard work matter, but they're not always enough to overcome the challenges that get thrown your way. Smart entrepreneurs know that planning gives them the competitive edge they need to dominate their market.

Don't Go Broke Before You Go Big

Many new entrepreneurs obsess over finding the perfect business idea when what they <u>really</u> should be worried about is running out of money. In fact, I have several friends and colleagues who got into business and learned quickly that it takes time for revenues to start flowing. In the meantime, most of them struggled under varying degrees of financial pressure.

And while statistics show that 20.4% of businesses fail in their first year and nearly half fail within five years, the business owners that beat these odds share a common trait: they've done their financial homework upfront and they know what they're getting into.

If you read the companion book to this business planner, *Your First Business Blueprint: How To Plan, Launch And Grow A Profitable Small Business*, you'll know that I'm a big fan of bootstrapping and retaining as much control over your business as possible. However, bootstrapping <u>does not</u> mean "winging it" financially and hoping for the best. It means being strategic about every dollar you spend and making sure you've got enough runway (a.k.a., how long a business can keep operating before it runs out of cash, assuming current income and expenses stay the same) to build something sustainable.

The entrepreneurs who succeed long-term understand their numbers from day one. They know how much money they need to start and keep things running and they're honest about just how long their savings will carry them as they build revenue. This transparency translates into a major advantage for business owners who can make confident decisions, focus on early growth and even take a few risks (if warranted) instead of constantly worrying about money.

Once you know where you stand financially, you can create a realistic plan that sets you up for success. You'll know exactly what you're working with, what you need and how to close any gaps between the two. I positioned this chapter before the actual business planning work for a simple reason: you can't create a realistic business plan if you don't know what resources you're working with.

It's Time for a Financial Gut Check

If you haven't taken a financial snapshot recently, this is a great time to do it. I've kept it simple, but if your financial picture is more complex you'll probably want to sit down with a financial planner or CPA to map out your own plan. I'll leave that part up to you, but for now let's do a basic reality check on where you stand financially.

Think of this as your financial pre-flight checklist. Airplane pilots don't take off without thoroughly checking their instruments and you shouldn't launch a business without understanding your money situation. This isn't about judgment or fear; it's about giving yourself the best possible chance to succeed.

Your Financial Gut Check Worksheet

Grab a calculator and be as honest as possible with your answers. No one else needs to see this, so no need to fudge the numbers or over/underestimate.

Your Current Resources:

- How much cash do you have in checking and savings right now? $_____

- How much do you have in other easily accessible accounts (money market, CDs, etc.)? $_____

- How much money does your spouse or significant other earn each month (if applicable)? $_____

- How much money can you reasonably expect to make during your first 6-12 months in business? $_____

Your Monthly Expenses (be thorough here):

- Mortgage or rent payment: $_____
- Car payments: $_____
- Credit card minimum payments: $_____
- Auto, home and other insurance: $_____
- Groceries and household items: $_____
- Utilities (electric, gas, water, trash): $_____
- Phone and internet: $_____
- Subscriptions (streaming, gym, etc.): $_____
- Your business startup costs (spread over 12 months): $_____
- Your business ongoing expenses (marketing, software, licenses): $_____
- Emergency fund contributions: $_____
- Other monthly obligations: $_____

Total Monthly Expenses: $_____

Next, take your total monthly expenses and subtract any income you'll have from other sources (spouse's salary, part-time job, etc.). This number tells you exactly how much money your business needs to generate each month just to keep you afloat.

Monthly income gap your business must fill: $_____

Use these numbers to create a simple monthly cash flow projection in Google Sheets or Excel. Update it every month as you learn more about your actual income and expenses. By mapping your financial landscape now, you're not just being transparent with yourself about potential challenges. You're building the foundation for sustainable success and giving yourself the clarity you need to make smart business decisions from day one.

The Financial Realities of Business Ownership

You know that sinking feeling when you drive by your favorite local ice cream shop, only to see an "Out of Business" sign haphazardly taped to the window? Or when you're craving that perfect slice from the little pizza place down the street, but Google Maps shows it as "Permanently Closed?"

We've all been there and the moment of disappointment isn't just about losing access to a favorite treat either. It's a stark reminder of how quickly businesses can close up shop, and often just when we thought they'd become a permanent part of our community.

The statistics on business failure tell a sobering story, but they also reveal clear patterns that smart entrepreneurs can learn from and avoid. While we regularly see businesses opening with great fanfare only to close their doors within months, the underlying causes are often predictable and preventable. That ice cream shop or pizza place didn't just vanish overnight; it likely struggled with the same fundamental challenges that impact thousands of businesses every year.

Why Businesses Fail: The Financial Factors

The most common culprits behind business failures are interconnected, but they all trace back to fundamental financial and planning oversights:

- **Poor financial planning and insufficient funding.** Startups often underestimate how much cash they need to operate before reaching profitability, leaving them scrambling when reality hits. This doesn't just apply to local restaurants either—it can happen to anyone in any type of business.
- **No solid business plan.** Without a clear roadmap, startups lack defined goals, strategies and a realistic understanding of challenges, leading to unfocused efforts that don't pay off.
- **Lack of market need.** Many businesses build products or services that nobody really needs or is willing to pay for, often because they skipped crucial market research before launching.
- **Marketing challenges.** Because even the coolest, most useful products won't generate revenue if customers don't know about them or understand their value.

To avoid these and other pitfalls, start by getting crystal clear on your current financial position by:

- **Detailing your startup costs.** Document everything you've spent or need to spend to get your business off the ground, including legal fees, equipment, initial inventory and website development.

- **Identifying your initial capital outlay.** Account for money you'll personally invest, any loans you need to secure and early investments you're seeking.

- **Tracking your burn rate.** Calculate how quickly you're spending capital each month <u>before</u> significant revenue begins flowing in (you'll want to keep doing this even as your company grows and especially if you're going to be taking on investors, who are very interested in this key indicator).

- **Listing out your revenue streams (and continually building new ones).** Include both existing income sources and anticipated future streams, even if they're still in development.

- **Separating your personal and business finances.** Use dedicated business bank accounts and credit cards from day one and implement simple tracking systems using spreadsheets or accounting software like QuickBooks, Xero or FreshBooks to keep close tabs on your business finances.

This financial clarity will help you make better decisions and gives your business the financial foundation it needs for long-term success. As you move forward with your business planning, remember that your data guides your strategy. Use financial insights like burn rate, revenue streams and costs to adapt quickly, prioritize efforts and allocate resources effectively.

Also, decisions should be rooted in numbers. Informed choices about pricing, hiring, marketing spend and even expansion should all be driven by your current financial reality and projections rather than gut feelings alone. And finally, your financial assessment isn't a *one-time report*; it's a continuous feedback loop that requires regular attention.

Let's Put Your Financial Data to Work

Now that you've documented your financial baseline, you can use the data to make smart, forward-looking decisions. For example:

> If your burn rate is high and your initial capital resources are limited, this tells you that you should focus intensely on generating revenue quickly or finding more funding.

> On the flip side, if a particular product or service is proving to be a stronger revenue stream than you anticipated, you might want to shift your marketing efforts or resources to double down on that success.

What's really exciting about having solid financial data is that it becomes your business GPS, guiding you toward the most profitable paths and helping you avoid costly detours. When your numbers reveal that you're spending $10,000 a month but bringing in $7,000, for example, you'll know to make some strategic (and hopefully temporary) changes before the issues turn into serious money problems. Think of it as an early warning system that gives you the power to course-correct while you have options.

Good financial tracking also helps you spot opportunities you might otherwise miss. Maybe you thought your main product would be your bread and butter, but the numbers show that your "side hustle" service is actually bringing in more profit with less effort. These and other pleasant surprises can completely reshape your business strategy and boost your bottom line without having to work twice as hard to get there.

 **MAKE THIS YOUR NEXT STEP**

Write down one financial goal that excites you about your business' future.

4 Quick Money Preservation Tips

- ☑ **Map your money**: Understand all initial investments & startup expenses.

- ☑ **Monitor cash flow:** Track your burn rate and identify revenue sources.

- ☑ **Establish boundaries:** Create separate business accounts (bank, credit, etc.).

- ☑ **Log every dollar:** Use simple tools to record all income and outgoing expenses.

2

STACK THE DECK IN YOUR FAVOR

Benjamin Franklin famously said, "If you fail to plan, you are planning to fail." Centuries later business coach Brian Tracy said: "Every minute you spend in planning saves you 10 minutes in execution and gives you a thousand percent return on your energy."

They were spoken hundreds of years apart, but these two statements point to the same truth: time spent planning <u>never goes to waste.</u> In fact, even minimal upfront effort can pay off by making your work faster, smoother and more efficient.

The numbers back this up. In the U.S., more than 5 million new businesses launch every year, creating both opportunity and intense competition. So how do you stand out in such a crowded landscape? Research shows that planning makes a real difference:

- → Entrepreneurs with business plans are 260% more likely to launch their companies.

- → A business plan increases the chances of growth by 30%.

- → About 70% of businesses that are 5+ years old follow a strategic plan.

- → 71% of fast-growing organizations reportedly have business plans in place.

- → Companies with written plans are 7% more likely to experience high growth.

- Just 35% of business owners ever develop a business plan, yet those who do are twice as likely to succeed.

- The message here is pretty clear: planning is more than just getting stuff down on paper. It's a proven way to boost your odds of not only getting your business off the ground but also running it with focus and discipline.

It's a Plan, Not the Great American Novel

You've probably seen those intimidating business plan templates that look like they were designed by someone who loves spreadsheets and has <u>way too much</u> time on their hands. They include sections for everything from your company's mission statement to your great-grandmother's recipe for success, complete with 47 different financial projections and a detailed analysis that requires a degree in acronym interpretation.

The truth is, you don't need to write The Great American Novel to create an effective business plan. You need the essential elements that actually matter, presented in a way that makes sense to real, busy humans. Focus on what works, skip the fluff and get your plan done so you can get back to actually running your business.

> Here are the seven core sections that belong in every solid business plan:
>
> **Executive Summary**: This is your business plan's elevator pitch that summarizes everything important in two pages or less.

Company Description: You'll explain what your business does, who it serves and what makes it different from other organizations.

Products and Services: This section details exactly what you're selling and why people will want to buy it.

Market Analysis: You'll research your industry, identify your target customers and size up the competition.

Marketing Strategy: Here's where you explain how you'll reach customers and convince them to choose you over the alternatives.

Financials: This covers your revenue projections, expense estimates and key financial assumptions.

Budget: You'll break down your startup costs, ongoing expenses and cash flow requirements to keep your business running.

The executive summary kicks things off with a compelling overview that's designed to capture attention and summarize your key points (think of it as your business plan's greatest hits album). The company description then dives deeper into your business's identity, mission and legal structure, while the products and services section outlines exactly what you're selling and how those things benefit your customers.

Your market analysis demonstrates your understanding of the industry, the target audience you'll be working with and your competitive landscape. The marketing strategy details how you'll reach and attract customers and your financials and budget section lays out the economic viability of your plan, along with projected income, expenses and funding needs.

Now, not everything you do is going to fit neatly into each one of these buckets. Conversely, not all of these sections cover every single thing that every individual entrepreneur needs in their plan and that's perfectly okay. This framework just provides a solid starting point and gives you the essential structure you need to build a personalized business plan that actually works for your specific situation.

 **MAKE THIS YOUR NEXT STEP**
Open a new doc and write "Executive Summary" at the top. You've just started your business plan.

4 Planning Hacks That Actually Work

☑ **Start with the essentials.** Focus on the seven core sections that matter and don't get bogged down trying to create a 50-page masterpiece that no one wants to read.

☑ **Remember the 260% advantage.** Entrepreneurs with business plans are reportedly 260% more likely to launch their companies, so you're literally improving your odds just by putting pen to paper.

☑ **Make it fit your business, not the template.** Your plan doesn't need to check every box in some generic framework, it needs to work for your specific situation and goals.

☑ **Think greatest hits, not encyclopedia.** Your executive summary should be like your business plan's greatest hits album, hitting the high notes in two pages or less.

3
YOUR INTERACTIVE BUSINESS PLAN WORKBOOK

Alright, entrepreneur! It's time to bust your business ideas out of your brain and onto paper with a tool that's actually interactive and fun to use. I've packed this workbook with a comprehensive framework covering 13 key areas, or basically everything you need to map out your success.

This isn't some dusty, generic textbook. I designed it specifically for new entrepreneurs and existing business owners like you, ensuring every element is directly applicable to your unique business.

So go ahead, dive in. Use this workbook to create a highly relevant and genuinely effective plan. Feel free to skip anything that genuinely doesn't apply to your venture, but trust me: the more thorough you are, the more power you'll unlock for your business.

Quick hint: Chapters 4 & 5 of this book include fully-completed sample plans for both product and services, so skip ahead and check those out if you want. Please use them for inspiration if you get stuck and to guide your planning journey.

1. **COVER SHEET.** This page should reflect the image of your new company and include any logos or graphics that you plan to use in your business. Use "Business Plan for Company" as the title and be sure to date the plan.

2. **TABLE OF CONTENTS.** For your own future reference and for anyone who will read your plan, you'll want to list each section and sub-section throughout the plan.

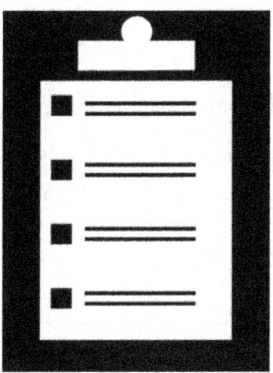

3. **EXECUTIVE SUMMARY.** This is a one- to two-page summary of your business plan, so you may want to write it after you've completed the rest of the document. Summarize the key points covered in the plan and include a complete-but-brief overview of your plan.

   You'll also want to discuss your new business and your goals. Here's an example: *"My business, [Your Business Name], will operate as an independent entity providing [Your Core Product/Service] to [Your Target Market]. My goal is to generate X amount of revenue, acquire X number of customers and/or produce X units annually, establish a strong market presence, build a loyal customer base and achieve sustainable growth."*

   Write your executive summary here: _____
   _____
   _____
   _____
   _____
   _____

4. **INDUSTRY/MARKET ANALYSIS:** When you write this section, assume that the person reading it knows nothing about you, your company or your industry. Make it as basic as possible and answer these questions.

How big is the industry? This is usually measured by data like the number of existing businesses already operating in your space, the size of the market opportunity, whether companies in the industry are growing or stagnating, etc.

_____
_____
_____
_____
_____
_____

How quickly is the industry growing? (Check out data generated by industry organizations and online reports from organizations like Statista or Markets and Markets for this information)

_____
_____
_____
_____
_____
_____

What are the typical profit margins? (Or, how much can you expect to pocket after overhead and expenses?)

_____
_____
_____
_____
_____
_____
_____

Who are the major players in the industry?

_____
_____
_____
_____
_____
_____
_____

What are some of the trends and forecasts for the industry? (Most national, state and local trade associations track and publish this type of market data)

_____
_____
_____
_____
_____

What changes are happening in the industry right now that will create new opportunities for companies like yours?

_____
_____
_____
_____
_____
_____

5. **BUSINESS OVERVIEW:** Describe the products or services that you'll be selling, how long your firm has been operating and a few of its short-term and long-term business goals. Focus on brief, concise descriptions in this section and keep it limited to one or two pages.

   Avoid using too much industry jargon and write this for someone who knows nothing about your industry. If you're going to use your business plan to seek financing or backing, you'll also want to detail what the funds will be used for (office equipment, vehicle, website development, first year's lease expenses, etc.). If you filled out the financial gut check worksheet in Chapter One you'll already have some of this information gathered.

Write your business overview here:

_____
_____

_____
_____
_____
_____

6. **OWNERSHIP & LEGAL STRUCTURE:** This will be the easy part since it's pretty common to launch as a sole proprietor. However, as your firm grows you'll probably reach a point where incorporating or starting a partnership may make sense. When this happens, you can adjust your plan to reflect these new realities and opportunities.

Capture your ownership and legal structure here:

_____
_____
_____
_____
_____

7. **MANAGEMENT & STAFF:** The good news is that when you stick with and put energy into growing your business, all of the duties outlined here won't fall on your shoulders forever. Soon, you'll be able to start hiring help to fuel your company's growth.

For now, start this section with a short paragraph detailing your own staffing aspirations (even if you're a one-person-show right now), describe what roles those team members or employees will fill in your growing business and detail your plans for adding human resources to your operation as it grows and prospers.

_____
_____
_____
_____
_____
_____

8. **MARKETING PLAN:** This section covers the fundamentals of how you'll connect your product or service with customers. It helps you clarify what you're selling, why people would want or need it and what value you provide. You'll outline how you plan to reach your target customers, how you'll conduct business with them and how you'll price your offerings. Here are some important details to consider and include:
    - → What you're selling
    - → Why customers want and/or need it
    - → What value you bring to the table
    - → How you will reach those customers
    - → How you will do business with those customers
    - → How your services will be priced
    - → What your competition looks like
    - → Your competitive advantage

Start capturing your marketing plan here:

_____
_____
_____
_____
_____
_____
_____

9. **OPERATIONAL PLAN:** Your operational plan outlines how your business will function day-to-day, and should include information about your location, facilities, equipment, staffing and key processes. You'll detail how you'll deliver your products or services, manage quality standards and handle customer service. This plan helps you identify potential bottlenecks before they become problems and ensures you have the infrastructure to support your business goals. Think about things like:
   - Who will run the business?
   - Where will the company be based?
   - Where will the work be done? (at the office, at home, at Starbucks)
   - The tools, resources and technology you'll use to work as efficiently as possible.
   - What tools or resources you'll need and which ones you already have to run the business.

What does your operational plan look like?

_____
_____
_____

10. **FINANCIAL PLAN:** Kick this section off with the words "level of funding needed to get my business going" and then document your needs. Develop an honest assessment of how much money you'll need to get this business off the ground and exactly how you'll use that money. If you have any historical financial statements (i.e., the past three years' balance sheets and income statements), include them. You'll also want to develop two to three years' worth of projections and forecasts for your new company. Remember, these projections can always be adjusted as you learn more about your market and operations, but for now they'll help you make informed decisions about funding and growth.

Start documenting your financial plan here:

_____
_____
_____
_____
_____
_____

11. **BUSINESS STRENGTHS AND WEAKNESS:** Use this space to talk about what's great and innovative about what you're doing, what makes you stand out in the marketplace and where you can use some help. Stick to three or four solid strengths that will make you stand out in the marketplace and be as specific as possible. Rather than using a statement like, "I provide great customer service" use specific language like: "I will empower small businesses in [a specific industry] with accessible technology solutions that streamline operations, fostering their growth and success in the digital age. Be equally as specific about any potentially weak areas and consider what steps you can take to address these issues.

Start by listing out your strengths here:

_____
_____
_____
_____
_____
_____

And then add any areas where you'd like to improve here:

_____
_____
_____
_____
_____
_____
_____

12. GROWTH PROJECTIONS: Developing your growth strategy is an exciting step. You're not just maintaining; you're actively building towards a bigger and brighter future for your business. Answering these questions will help you formulate growth projections for your new or expanding enterprise.

Where do I see my company and myself in one year?

_____
_____
_____
_____
_____
_____
_____

Where will I be in five years?

_____
_____

And, how will I get where I want to go? (e.g., strategies, tactics, growth plans, etc.)

Are these goals realistically attainable in my industry? Do some research, talk to other entrepreneurs in your field and form a consensus based on input from a variety of different sources.

Can my market support these growth projections? Research your market, look at how many new businesses enter the sector each year, how the customer base and its needs are changing, etc.

_____
_____
_____
_____
_____
_____

What new customer niches can I tap into and cultivate in order to reach my goals? Brainstorm some ideas here.

_____
_____
_____
_____
_____
_____
_____

How much can I reasonably expect my sales to grow each year with this plan in place?

_____
_____
_____
_____

_____

_____

_____

13. **EXIT STRATEGY:** Any business expert will tell you that having a Plan B and even a Plan C in place can mean the difference between success and failure in the competitive business landscape. Creating an exit strategy early in the process doesn't mean you're ready to give up; it means you're ready to embrace anything that comes your way and treat your practice like a business and not a hobby.

"An exit strategy is critical, but it's something that very few entrepreneurs think about when they're writing their first business plan," says one college professor who teaches entrepreneurship. "They're so concerned with getting their companies off the ground and making payroll, that they overlook the need for an exit strategy."

What will your exit strategy look like? Start capturing it here:

_____

_____

_____

_____

_____

_____

_____

_____

_____

This workbook isn't a test that you have to ace on the first try, and you don't have to fill in <u>every single section</u> perfectly before moving forward with your business idea. Think of it as more of a "living document" that grows right along with your business. Kick it off with what you know today, make your best educated guesses and leave some sections blank if you need to. The goal is not perfection; it's progress.

Beyond the Basics: Optional Sections That Add Value

Depending on what type of business you're starting, you may want to include additional elements that strengthen your plan. These extras provide more depth for investors, lenders or simply for your own strategic planning.

> - **Legal protections.** Document any licenses, trademarks or copyrights that protect your business or intellectual property.
>
> - **Timelines for major milestones.** Outline the timing of significant operations like business expansion, hiring employees, team formation or launching your online presence.
>
> - **Key business assumptions.** Include anticipated sales volume, cost of goods sold, gross profit margins and relevant data from trade associations.
>
> - **Detailed income projections.** Provide monthly

projections for three to five years, then quarterly projections for the following three to five years.

- **Cash flow statements.** Show monthly cash flow for two years and then quarterly projections for three to five additional years.

- **Breakeven analysis.** Calculate exactly when your business will reach profitability, which can range from 2-3 months for some to 3-5 years (or even longer in some cases) for others.

A Map for Handling the Twists, Turns and Roadblocks

Congratulations! By completing this workbook, you've taken a giant step toward actually knowing what you're doing, which already puts you ahead of any entrepreneur who is just winging it. Remember that this business plan isn't a static document you'll stuff in a drawer and forget about. It's a living blueprint that you can revisit, refine and use to guide your decisions when things get interesting.

The journey of successful business ownership is rarely a straight line, but with a well-defined plan in hand, you'll be able to handle those inevitable curves, detours and the occasional pothole that life throws your way. Stay committed to your goals, consistently review your progress and adapt your strategies as needed. You've got the power to build something amazing and this business plan is the strategic tool that will help you get there.

> 👉 **MAKE THIS YOUR NEXT STEP**
>
> *Start by answering just one question in the workbook.*
> *It doesn't have to be perfect, it just has to be started.*

4 Ways to Gain a Planning Edge

☑ **Start with what you know, guess where you don't.** You don't need perfect information to begin planning, just make your best educated guesses and fill in the blanks as you learn more about your business.

☑ **Think living document, not final exam.** Your business plan should grow and evolve with your understanding, so revisit and refine it regularly instead of treating it like a one-and-done assignment.

☑ **Skip what doesn't fit, but don't ignore the hard stuff.** Feel free to leave out sections that genuinely don't apply to your venture, but tackle the challenging parts because that's where the real value lies.

☑ **Use the samples when you're stuck.** Check out the completed examples in Chapters 4 and 5 of this book for inspiration and guidance when you hit a roadblock in your planning process.

4

SERVICE BUSINESS PLAN BLUEPRINT

Building a comprehensive business plan from the ground up takes focus, dedication and thoughtful planning. Here's a complete service-focused business plan example (excluding the cover sheet & table of contents, which you'll create after you finalize your own draft) to serve as your roadmap, inspiration source and reference guide when you need extra direction on specific sections.

This numbered list aligns with the one you'll find in the business planning workbook in Chapter 3.

1. **COVER SHEET**
2. **TABLE OF CONTENTS**
3. **EXECUTIVE SUMMARY**

Sean Andrews is an aspiring entrepreneur who wants to launch a mobile auto detailing business serving his immediate local area. With five years of experience in the automotive field and a strong passion for automotive aesthetics, he wants to provide high-quality, convenient detailing services directly to clients' homes or workplaces.

While Sean may be new to formal business ownership, he possesses a strong work ethic and a keen eye for detail honed through relevant past experiences, his own personal car care and a previous job requiring meticulousness. He's proficient with scheduling apps, payment processing and social media, all of which will play an important role in his mobile business.

The new company will offer a range of on-demand auto detailing services, from basic washes and interior cleanings to premium paint corrections and ceramic coatings. Pricing will be competitive, reflecting the convenience and quality of a mobile service, with potential for tiered packages and subscription options.

4. INDUSTRY/MARKET ANALYSIS

The Overall Market
The auto detailing market in Sean's area is dynamic, with a mix of brick-and-mortar detail shops, car washes offering detailing services and a growing number of mobile operators. While established players exist, there's room for a new mobile service that prioritizes convenience, personalized attention and high-quality results. The overall market is supported by a strong car culture and consumers who value their vehicles, seeking to maintain their appearance and protect their investment.

Changes in the Market
The auto detailing industry has seen a notable shift towards mobile services, driven by consumer demand for convenience and time-saving solutions. Advanced detailing products and techniques (e.g., ceramic coatings, paint correction) are also gaining popularity, creating opportunities for businesses offering specialized services. Furthermore, increased environmental awareness means demand for eco-friendly products and water-conscious detailing methods is growing. The rise of ride-sharing services and car subscriptions also creates a niche for fleet maintenance.

Target Market and Customers

Initially, Sean will focus on residential neighborhoods with homeowners, affluent communities, business parks, busy professionals and classic car owners. His target customers include (but aren't limited to):

- Busy professionals and families who value convenience and saving time by having their cars detailed at home or work.
- Car enthusiasts who are willing to pay for premium services to maintain their vehicles' pristine condition.
- Small business owners who may need fleet detailing for company vehicles.
- Individuals with limited mobility who benefit from a mobile service.

Nature of Competition

Competition in the mobile auto detailing market comes from several different sources, including:

- Established brick-and-mortar detail shops that offer comprehensive services but lack the convenience of mobile.
- Other mobile detailers offering different price, quality and service offerings.
- Automated car washes that provide quick, low-cost options but often lack the thoroughness of hand detailing.
- "Do-it-yourself" car owners who prefer to clean their own vehicles, often with varying results.

Opportunities

For a mobile auto detailing business focused on quality and convenience, the opportunity areas include:

- Busy lifestyles mean more people are willing to pay for services delivered to them. Targeting high-end vehicles, classic cars or commercial fleets.
- Collaborating with auto dealerships, body shops, car rental companies or even local businesses (e.g., gyms, office complexes) for onsite detailing events.
- Offering recurring detailing services to ensure steady income

5. BUSINESS OVERVIEW

By providing top-tier, convenient and reliable auto detailing services directly to clients, Sean will help customers enhance the longevity and appearance of their vehicles, saving them time and effort. His core business mission is to deliver exceptional customer satisfaction through meticulous work and a professional, friendly approach.

To hit these goals, Sean will continuously invest in high-quality, professional-grade equipment and eco-friendly products, stay updated on the latest detailing techniques and ensure every vehicle receives personalized attention and care. Sean's focus is on building a reputation as the go-to mobile detailer in his surrounding area.

6. OWNERSHIP AND LEGAL STRUCTURE

Sean will initially operate as a sole proprietor. This structure offers simplicity in setup and taxation. As the business grows and profitability increases, he can consult with an accountant to assess the benefits of transitioning to an LLC (Limited Liability Company) to mitigate personal liability and explore potential tax advantages or a Subchapter S Corporation for pass-through taxation. For now, sole proprietorship is the most straightforward choice. He will also need the proper licenses and/or insurance coverage particularly because he will be cleaning other people's physical property.

7. MANAGEMENT AND STAFFING

As a new mobile auto detailing business owner, Sean will be the primary operator, responsible for all detailing work, customer communication, scheduling, marketing and administrative tasks. Until consistent business volume warrants additional hands on deck, Sean will handle all aspects of his business himself. Future plans include the potential for hiring a part-time assistant for administrative tasks, marketing support or eventually, additional detailers as the client base expands significantly.

8. MARKETING PLAN

Sean's initial marketing efforts will focus on building a strong local presence and generating referrals. Some of the strategies he'll want to use include:

Sales Tactics
- A user-friendly web platform or app for scheduling appointments, showcasing services and displaying pricing.
- Discounts or incentives for existing customers who refer new clients.
- Collaboration with local car washes (for overflow detailing), tire shops, auto mechanics or dealerships.
- Connecting with potential clients in affluent neighborhoods, business parks or specific car communities (e.g., classic car clubs).

Advertising
- Using platforms like Instagram and Facebook to showcase work with visually appealing before- and-after photos/videos, run targeted ads and engage with the local community.
- Optimizing his business website and Google My Business profile for local search terms (e.g., "mobile auto detailing in Tulsa, Okla.")
- Targeted Google or Facebook ads to reach potential customers searching for detailing services on the socials.

Promotions and Publicity
- Introductory discounts or package deals to attract initial customers.
- Themed detailing packages for different times of the year (e.g., "Spring Refresh," "Winter Protection").
- Press releases sent to local community newspapers

or digital outlets announcing the launch and unique selling proposition of the mobile service.
- Actively encouraging satisfied customers to leave positive reviews on Google, Yelp and social media platforms.

9. OPERATIONAL PLAN

Sean's operational plan will focus on efficiency, quality control and seamless service delivery. To get going, he'll need:

- A professional-grade mobile detailing setup, including a water tank, pressure washer, vacuum, steam cleaner and a full range of high-quality detailing chemicals, tools and microfiber towels.
- A system for managing appointments, optimizing routes and ensuring timely arrival at client locations.
- A standardized, efficient detailing process for each service package to ensure consistent quality and minimize time spent onsite.
- A well-stocked inventory of supplies and track usage to prevent running out of essential products.
- Clear communication protocols for booking, confirming appointments and providing post-service follow-up.

10. FINANCIAL PLAN

Sean has 12 months of personal savings to cover initial startup costs and living expenses during the early stages of his business.

The goal is to become profitable within 12 months of launching his new business. He'll do this by:

- Developing tiered pricing for different detailing packages and individual services, ensuring profitability while remaining competitive.

- Recording and keeping close tabs on all startup costs (e.g., equipment, supplies, vehicle modifications, insurance) and ongoing operational expenses (e.g., fuel, supplies, marketing, software subscriptions).

- Establishing realistic monthly and quarterly revenue goals based on service capacity and anticipated bookings.

- Monitoring cash inflows and outflows closely to ensure sufficient working capital.

- Developing detailed sales forecasts, profit and loss statements and cash flow projections for the first 1-3 years.

11. BUSINESS STRENGTHS AND WEAKNESSES

Key Competitive Capabilities

The mobile nature of Sean's new business speaks directly to growing customer demand for on-demand services that save them time, effort and hassle. As a sole operator initially, Sean can offer highly personalized attention and build strong customer relationships. A dedication to meticulous work and the use of premium products will help him differentiate his business from lower-quality competitors. Sean's genuine enthusiasm for automotive care translates into high-quality work and a positive customer experience.

Key Competitive Weaknesses
Limited initial capital might restrict the speed of equipment acquisition or marketing efforts. Building trust and awareness in a competitive market will take time and consistent effort. At least in the beginning, all operational tasks fall on Sean's shoulders. This could potentially lead to long hours or burnout if not managed effectively. Outdoor work like auto detailing is also impacted by adverse weather conditions and often requires flexible scheduling and potential indoor alternatives (if available).

12. GROWTH PROJECTIONS

In the first year, Sean's primary focus will be on establishing a strong foundation, building a loyal customer base and refining operational efficiency. The goal is to achieve an average of 3-5 bookings per week by the end of the first six months, leading to 10-15 consistent clients per week by year end. He'll get there by:

- Consistently delivering high-quality service to drive repeat business and positive reviews. Actively marketing through social media and local partnerships.
- Building a strong referral network.
- Achieving profitability within 12 months.

Over the following five years, Sean envisions strategic growth and expansion. His initial goals include:

Years 2-3: Consistently service [e.g., 15-20 vehicles per week], potentially adding specialized services (e.g., marine detailing, RVs, commercial fleets) and exploring a part-time administrative assistant to manage scheduling and marketing.

Years 4-5: Consider acquiring a second fully equipped detailing vehicle and hiring the first full-time detailer to expand capacity and geographic reach or explore a subscription-based model for recurring revenue. The aim is to establish his company as a leading mobile detailing service in the region.

13. EXIT STRATEGY

As a brand new business owner, Sean's immediate focus is on building a robust and profitable mobile auto detailing service, but he's also going to be creating a valuable asset that may be saleable in the future. His potential exit strategies could include:

- Selling the business: Once established with a loyal customer base and proven profitability, the business could be sold to another entrepreneur looking to enter the mobile detailing market. The salable assets include the company's client list, equipment and established brand reputation.

- Merging with a larger detailing shop: A successful mobile operation could be an attractive acquisition for a larger brick-and-mortar detailing business looking to expand its service offerings.

- Transition to a management role: If the business grows to include multiple detailers, Sean could eventually transition out of hands-on detailing into a purely management and oversight role.

 MAKE THIS YOUR NEXT STEP

Borrow one idea from the sample plan that you'd like to adapt for your own business.

5

BUILD YOUR PRODUCT PLAN

Creating a new business plan from scratch takes time, effort and mental energy. Here's a sample product-focused business plan (minus the cover sheet & table of contents, which you can develop once you have your plan framed out) that you can use as a guide, for ideas and to help you work through sections where you might need a bit more inspiration.

This numbered list aligns with the one you'll find in the business planning workbook in Chapter 3.

1. **COVER SHEET**
2. **TABLE OF CONTENTS**
3. **EXECUTIVE SUMMARY**

Brenda Hart is launching a new online subscription box business aimed at busy professionals, eco-conscious consumers and hobbyists. This venture will leverage the founder's experience in e-commerce and niche product curation and passion for gourmet foods and snacks that are made by environmentally conscious companies.

The subscription box model offers a recurring revenue stream and caters to a growing consumer demand for curated, convenient and surprise-filled product experiences delivered directly to their door. Brenda will focus on competitive pricing, unique themes and her vendors' strong environmental, governance and sustainability (ESG) commitments to stand out in the crowded subscription box market.

Initial efforts will involve sourcing products, building the e-commerce platform, developing marketing strategies and engaging with early adopters to secure the early subscribers within the first 60-90 days. The goal is to establish a strong brand identity, optimize the customer acquisition funnel and achieve sustained subscriber growth.

4. INDUSTRY/MARKET ANALYSIS

The Overall Market
The online subscription box market is a rapidly expanding segment within e-commerce, driven by consumers' desire for convenience, discovery and curated experiences. It spans various categories, including beauty, food, fashion, pets and hobbies. While competitive, the market continues to grow, indicating significant opportunities for niche players like Brenda, who can identify and serve underserved segments or offer truly unique value propositions. Growth in this segment is also fueled by social media trends, influencer marketing and the fact that more and more people are buying online.

Changes in the Market
Recent trends in the subscription box market include a move towards greater personalization, increased demand for sustainable and ethically sourced products and the rise of niche boxes targeting very specific interests. Consumers are also becoming more discerning, valuing transparency in product sourcing and a seamless unboxing experience. The e-commerce surge has solidified online purchasing habits, further benefiting subscription services.

Target Market and Customers

Brenda will target consumers who want to sample and enjoy new products but who don't have the time or energy to shop in person for these types of products, which are often limited to niche stores and/or gourmet shops. Her target market is active online, often engages with social media and is comfortable with recurring payments for services that enhance their lifestyle or interests.

Nature of Competition

The online subscription box industry includes large, established players and many other smaller, highly specialized niche boxes. Competition comes from direct competitors (other subscription boxes in the same category), indirect competitors (traditional retail stores, one-time online purchases) and even DIY options where customers assemble similar products themselves. Key competitive factors include product curation quality, pricing, marketing effectiveness, brand loyalty and customer service.

Competitors

Brenda can do some online research see which companies are already operating in her specific subscription box space and shouldn't be deterred by direct online retailers already selling similar products. In many cases, this is more an indicator of demand than a deterrent for new entrants into the market.

Opportunities

Significant opportunities exist for subscription box providers that can:

- Deeply personalize content: Leveraging data to offer highly tailored boxes.

- Focus on underserved niches: Identifying communities with specific interests not yet fully catered to.
- Emphasize sustainability and ethical sourcing: Appealing to conscious consumers.
- Create a strong community: Building engagement beyond the box itself through online forums, exclusive content or events.
- Offer exceptional unboxing experiences: Elevating the physical delivery of the box.

5. BUSINESS OVERVIEW

Brenda wants to offer an enticing and convenient way for busy individuals to discover artisanal, unique and eco-conscious products from around the world. By offering expertly curated products, exceptional customer service and a memorable unboxing experience, she'll cultivate a loyal subscriber base and establish her firm as a leading brand in her specific market. Her focus will be on consistently delivering value, fostering a sense of community and continually innovating her product offerings.

6. OWNERSHIP AND LEGAL STRUCTURE

Brenda will initially operate as a sole proprietor but she has her sights set on growth and expansion. This structure offers simplicity in setup and taxation for initial operations. As the business grows and achieves profitability, she can consult with a business attorney and accountant to evaluate transitioning to a Limited Liability Company (LLC) for personal liability protection or potentially a Subchapter S Corporation for potential tax advantages, based on projected revenue and legal advice.

7. MANAGEMENT AND STAFFING

This new product-based business will initially be solely managed and operated by Brenda, who will handle all aspects of the business, including product sourcing, web management, marketing, customer service, packing and shipping. As the subscriber base grows, she'll prioritize hiring part-time or full-time staff for key operational areas such as fulfillment, customer support and marketing assistance. She'll also look for new ways to collaborate with freelancers or agencies on specialized tasks like graphic design or advanced digital marketing. This will help Brenda scale her business without having to hire full- or part-time help, at least in the early stages.

8. MARKETING PLAN

Brenda's initial marketing efforts will focus on building brand awareness and acquiring early subscribers using this multi-channel approach:

Sales Tactics
- Influencer Marketing: Partnering with relevant micro- and macro-influencers on platforms like Instagram, TikTok and YouTube to showcase unboxing experiences and drive traffic.
- Content Marketing: Creating engaging blog posts,

videos and social content related to the box's theme, offering value and attracting organic traffic.
- Email Marketing: Building an email list pre-launch and post-launch to nurture leads, announce new boxes and promote special offers.
- Referral Programs: Incentivizing existing subscribers to refer new customers.
- Limited-Time Offers/Bundles: Creating urgency and value for new subscribers.

Advertising
- Social Ads: Targeted campaigns on platforms like Facebook and Instagram, utilizing demographic and interest-based targeting to reach ideal customers.
- Search Engine Marketing (SEM): Pay-per-click (PPC) campaigns on Google, targeting keywords related to subscription boxes and the niche.
- Partnerships: Collaborating with complementary brands or niche online communities for cross-promotional opportunities.

Promotions and Publicity
- Launch Press Release: Announcing the official launch of [Subscription Box Name] to relevant online publications, blogs and industry journalists.
- Unboxing Videos/Reviews: Encouraging and featuring customer-generated unboxing videos and reviews on social media and the website.
- Giveaways and Contests: Running promotional giveaways to generate buzz and grow the email list/social media following.

- Affiliate Marketing: Partnering with websites and content creators to promote the box in exchange for a commission on sales.

9. OPERATIONAL PLAN

The operational backbone of Brenda's new company will center on efficient product sourcing, meticulous curation, streamlined fulfillment and responsive customer service. She'll establish relationships with reliable suppliers and artisans for high-quality, unique products that align with the box's theme. A robust vetting process will ensure product quality and ethical sourcing.

Brenda will also use an e-commerce storefront platform like Shopify and a subscription app like Recharge for website hosting, order management and subscription billing. Inventory management software will be integrated to track stock levels. She'll also implement systems to forecast demand, manage inventory levels and minimize waste or stock-outs.

10. FINANCIAL PLAN

Brenda has enough personal savings and available personal credit to cover her initial startup costs, including web development, initial inventory purchases, marketing expenses and operating overhead for the first 3-6 months. Her primary goal is to achieve profitability within 12 months by reaching a target subscriber base and optimizing her cost of goods sold (COGS) and operational expenses.

Using a system like QuickBooks or FreshBooks, Brenda will be able to handle the accounting, expense tracking and invoicing for her new company. She'll do regular reviews of profit & loss statements, balance sheets and cash flow projections to make more informed decisions.

11. BUSINESS STRENGTHS AND WEAKNESSES

Key Competitive Capabilities
- Deep understanding and passion for the specific product niche and a knack for curating great products for the boxes.
- Ability to leverage digital marketing and social media effectively to reach the target audience.
- Commitment to delivering exceptional customer service and a delightful unboxing experience.
- Minimal overhead initially to maximize profitability and flexibility.

Key Competitive Weaknesses
- Limited Brand Recognition: As a new entrant, building trust and recognition will take time and consistent effort.
- Initial manual processes may become bottlenecks as subscriber numbers grow, requiring significant investment in automation or outsourcing.
- Reliance on external suppliers for products can introduce risks related to quality, consistency and timely delivery.

- The subscription model creates recurring revenue but still requires careful management of upfront inventory costs versus staggered revenue.

12. GROWTH PROJECTIONS

In the first year, Brenda will be establishing a strong foundation for sustained growth. She'll actively seek customer feedback to iterate on box themes and product selection. Weekly dedication to targeted digital advertising, influencer collaborations and email list growth will be crucial to meeting these goals.

For the next five years, Brenda's operational plan involves strategic expansion and diversification. By year five, she wants to have a consistent base of active subscribers in place, potentially launching new box variations or one-time product offerings. She'll also explore automating fulfillment processes, expanding her marketing channels (e.g., podcast sponsorships, Pinterest ads) and potentially hiring dedicated roles for customer success and content creation to support growth and maintain high customer service levels (which, in this type of business, translates into a steady stream of referrals, positive reviews and new customers).

13. EXIT STRATEGY

As a new online subscription box business owner, Brenda's initial focus is on building a sustainable and profitable business with a loyal subscriber base. However, understanding the long-term vision is crucial. Her ultimate goal is to create a valuable asset that offers flexibility and financial security.

With this in mind, her potential exit strategies may include:

- Selling the entire business (e.g., brand, subscriber list, supplier relationships, website) to a larger company looking to expand into the subscription box market or its specific niche.
- Joining forces with another online business that targets a similar audience but offers different products, creating a more comprehensive offering.
- Potentially selling the recurring subscriber list or key assets like intellectual property (e.g., curation methodology, brand guidelines) to another operator.

>  **MAKE THIS YOUR NEXT STEP**
>
> *Use something you learned from the sample plan to make one small improvement to your own draft plan.*

6

DON'T FILE YOUR PLAN AWAY. ACTIVATE IT!

You've just spent all that time creating your business plan, and now you're probably thinking you can check "business planning" off your entrepreneurial to-do list and move on to the next phase, right?

Hold on a minute: Creating your plan was just the beginning. The real work starts when you actually put that plan to work instead of letting it sit unused in some folder on your computer.

Business plans aren't meant to be <u>static documents that you create once and then file away</u>. They're working documents that require regular attention, updates and adjustments. Your plan should guide your daily decisions and help you navigate challenges, not gather dust while you wing it through your business operations.

Look at your plan like a strategic compass that will help you make informed decisions, track your progress and adapt to changing marketplace conditions. You can use your plan to:

- Guide your daily operational decisions
- Attract and align team members
- Track progress towards goals
- Identify and avoid potential risks
- Validate some new business ideas
- Secure funding from outside investors
- Establish pricing strategies and adjust them based on market feedback
- Plan for seasonal fluctuations or industry cycles
- Evaluate partnership and expansion opportunities
- Communicate your vision clearly to stakeholders
- Set realistic timelines for major milestones

So as you can see, business planning is about more than just setting targets. It's about applying the insights you've gained, communicating your vision and consistently measuring your performance against the benchmarks that you've established. This is critical because markets shift, new opportunities come up and fresh challenges appear. Your plan should grow with your business.

Now, this doesn't mean you need to change your plan from week to week, but I do recommend reviewing it and freshening it up (if warranted) every quarter during your first couple of years in business. Those regular check-ins keep your plan relevant and help you stay focused on what matters most. Keep your business plan flexible, keep it current and let it be a consistent reminder of why you started this journey in the first place.

Your Annual Growth Check-In

Once your business finds its rhythm, you can shift away from doing quarterly reviews and over to annual planning sessions. Treat this like a non-negotiable meeting with yourself (or with key stakeholders, if you have some). You don't have to rewrite your plan from scratch. Just update it to match your progress and where you want to go next. Here's a simple 5-step framework you can use for your annual growth check-ins:

- **Block the time for it.** Reserve a half or full day once a year. No excuses!
- **Review your plan.** Print it or pull it up and walk through every section.
- **Check progress.** Compare results against last year's goals.

> → **Make updates.** Adjust what's no longer working and refine what is.
> → **Set goals.** Record your top priorities for the next 12 months.

Follow through on this and you'll have a business plan that pays dividends by keeping you on track, helping you work through challenges and identifying new opportunities before your competitors spot them.

Your Success Journey Starts Here

Congratulations! You've done something that puts you ahead of most people who talk about starting a business: you actually created a plan of action for yourself. When opportunities show up or problems arise, you won't be flying blind. You'll have a roadmap to guide your decisions and keep you focused on what really matters.

Stay committed to your vision, keep your plan updated and don't let small setbacks derail your bigger goals. You've got the tools and the knowledge to make this work. Now go out there and prove it to yourself.

The stage is set. Now go build something amazing!

☞ **MAKE THIS YOUR NEXT STEP**

Block 30 minutes on your calendar today for your first quarterly plan review.

Four Winning Ways to Maximize Your Planning Investment

☑ **Treat your plan like a living document.** Adapt it to market changes and new opportunities.

☑ **Schedule quarterly reviews, especially early on.** Regularly assess and refine your plan during your first few years when everything changes rapidly and you're learning the most.

☑ **Switch to annual reviews once you find your rhythm.** At that point, commit to reviewing your plan annually against your goals and making necessary adjustments.

☑ **Use your reviews to spot what's actually working.** Don't just focus on what needs fixing. Identify your wins and double down on the strategies that drive real results.

7

10 BONUS TIPS FOR BUSINESS PLANNING SUCCESS

Every successful enterprise starts with more than just a brilliant concept. It takes strategy to navigate challenges and seize opportunities. Throughout this book, I've outlined the key pillars that help startups build a solid foundation, attract customers, manage finances and achieve sustainable growth.

Now it's time for final words of wisdom to put your business plan into action. Whether you're ready to launch or haven't filled in your business plan yet, this is your moment. These bonus tips will help you cross the finish line and get moving.

1. Your Plan Should Guide, Not Control. Create a plan that guides your decisions and that doesn't restrict your creativity, ingenuity and innovation. When opportunities arise that align with your goals, grab 'em! Smart entrepreneurs use plans as strategic frameworks, not rigid rulebooks.

2. Prioritize Sales Early On. Your business needs cash flow to survive and thrive, so don't try to perfect every detail before you start selling. Identify your quickest path to revenue and prioritize activities that directly contribute to making sales.

3. Know Your Numbers. Track these three key metrics: how much you're bringing in, how much you're spending, and what's left over.

4. Test Small First. Before investing too heavily in marketing, inventory or equipment, run small tests to validate your assumptions. This saves money and will help you determine what actually works (and, what doesn't).

5. Build Customers Before Infrastructure. Don't spend on fancy offices, elaborate websites or expensive equipment until you know that customers will pay for what you're selling.

6. Solve Real Customer Problems. The most successful businesses address genuine pain points that customers actively want to solve. For example, Uber helps streamline transportation, Airbnb helps us avoid expensive hotel stays and Slack addresses email overload.

7. Price Based on Value, Not Costs. Set your prices according to the value you provide to customers, not just delivery costs (or, the time you spent working on their project). Think about the deliverable: if your solution saves someone $10,000, charging $2,000 for your product or service is reasonable regardless of your actual costs.

8. Document What Works. When you find marketing messages that convert, sales processes that close deals or operational procedures that save time, write them down. That way you can refer back to them and use them again instead of reinventing the wheel every time.

9. Network with Purpose. Attend industry events (both online and offline) with specific goals. Are you looking for customers, partners, mentors or suppliers? Targeted networking produces better results than just random schmoozing and registering for webinars that don't add value.

10. Build for the Success That's Coming Your Way. Successful entrepreneurs don't just plan to get by, they build systems designed to thrive when demand takes off. Design your business to handle sustainable, long-term success, not just survive the startup phase.

Your Next Steps Start Now

You've invested time in learning how to create an effective business plan. Now comes the part that separates successful entrepreneurs from those who just talk about starting businesses: execution.

Your plan gives you the roadmap.

And speaking of roadmaps, if you'd like some more help starting and/or growing your new business, definitely check out my other book, *Your First Business Blueprint: How To Plan, Launch And Grow A Profitable Small Business.* It gives you everything you need to know to confidently launch, run and grow a business in today's marketplace.

Whether you use this book alone or combine it with the *Blueprint*, you now have what you need to succeed. It's time to stop planning and start doing. Your business is waiting!

Startup Resource Hub

Starting a small business means a lot of learning and finding the right tools to make the process easier. To make things simpler, I've put together a list of resources you can use as you get your business off the ground. This list of resources was compiled based on my own research and several other curated resource lists published by the U.S. Chamber of Commerce, S.C.O.R.E and startup savant.

This list is for your information only. I'm not affiliated with any of these sites or tools. They're simply options you can explore as you move through the early stages of business ownership.

Want the clickable version? You'll find the full list with live links online at: bridgetmccrea.com/startup-resources

SUPPORT FOR SMALL BUSINESS OWNERS

National Association for the Self-Employed (NASE)
NASE.org
NASE represents companies with 10 employees or fewer. It offers free resources for small business owners and more tools for members, including unlimited access to consultants for tax, retirement, finance and operations questions. NASE also provides a member-only NASE Succeed Scholarship, helping entrepreneurs pay for training programs, business courses and college.

U.S. Small Business Administration (SBA)
SBA.gov

The SBA offers informative content, interactive online tools and a video library for entrepreneurs. These range from business planning solutions to mentoring services and include:

- Small Business Development Centers: Attend in-person events and get individualized assistance from small business centers near you.
- SBA's Ascent: A free online learning platform designed specifically to help women entrepreneurs start, grow and expand their businesses.
- Learning center courses: The SBA's learning center video courses cover starting up to selling your business and everything in between.
- Boots to Business: If you're a transitioning service member (including National Guard and Reserve) or a spouse with access to a military installation, check out the Boots to Business program.

Service Corps of Retired Executives (SCORE)
SCORE.org

SCORE provides resources for small business owners, including webinars, interactive courses, business templates and local workshops. For example, SCORE's Startup Roadmap guides individuals who are starting a new business. An entrepreneur can complete the 12-module step-by-step tutorial alone or with a mentor.

U.S. Chamber of Commerce

Uschamber.com

As the world's largest business organization, the U.S. Chamber of Commerce advocates for business-friendly policies and provides free resources for entrepreneurs. You'll find many virtual events and informative guides on small business topics and can network within your community by joining a local branch (you can use this directory to find your local Chamber of Commerce).

Minority Business Development Agency (MBDA)

MBDA.gov

The agency supports businesses in minority communities by providing grant and loan information, business opportunities and business certification resources. It links minority-owned businesses with the capital, contracts and markets they need to grow. The MBDA also advocates and promotes minority-owned business with elected officials, policy makers and business leaders.

Small Business Development Centers (SBDC)

sba.gov/local-assistance/resource-partners/small-business-development-centers-sbdc

This is a nationwide network, often hosted by universities and colleges, that provides free, confidential business consulting and low-cost training to entrepreneurs and small business owners. Funded in part by the SBA, SBDCs offer a wide range of assistance from business plan development and financial management to marketing and access to capital, aiming to promote small business growth and contribute to the economy.

National Federation of Independent Businesses (NFIB)
NFIB.com
NFIB is a non-profit organization that serves as the voice of small and independent businesses in the United States. It advocates for the interests of its members, representing them in Washington, D.C. and all 50 state capitals. The organization provides resources, research and legal support to help small businesses thrive.

FINANCIAL, LEGAL AND TAX SUPPORT

FDIC: Money Smart for Small Business
Fdic.gov/consumer-resource-center/money-smart-small-business
Boost your financial literacy with 13 modules for starting and managing a business. The materials and instructor-led curriculum were developed jointly by the Small Business Administration and Federal Deposit Insurance Corporation (FDIC). You can download financial resources right from the catalog, which is online here.

IRS Small Business and Self-Employed Tax Center
Irs.gov/businesses/small-businesses-self-employed
Get answers to your small business tax questions at the IRS Small Business and Self-Employed Tax Center. It provides free resources for taxpayers who file Form 1040 or 1040-SR and small companies with assets under $10 million. Some of the key topics covered include tax prep,
filing/paying taxes and the stages of business ownership.

Nav
Nav.com
Nav is a financial health platform for small businesses. It allows

entrepreneurs to see potential financing options they may qualify for before applying. For instance, a business owner signs up for a free account and inputs business data (like credit history and bank transactions). Then, Nav compares your information against funding requirements from more than 200 partners.

Find Law
Findlaw.com
FindLaw is an online legal resource and a platform that business owners and others can use to connect with legal professionals. It offers a library of free, accessible legal information on various business topics, from choosing a business structure and intellectual property to contracts and tax obligations.

LegalZoom
Legalzoom.com
LegalZoom provides online legal solutions for small businesses and individuals, making it easier to form various business entities like LLCs and corporations, register trademarks and draft legal documents.

ZenBusiness
Zenbusiness.com
ZenBusiness offers streamlined services for forming LLCs, corporations and other business structures. Its goal is to simplify the legal and administrative steps involved in starting a business, including registered agent services, operating agreement templates and compliance assistance.

ACCOUNTING & FINANCIAL MANAGEMENT

QuickBooks

Quickbooks.com

QuickBooks is a widely used accounting software for small businesses. It helps manage income and expenses, track sales, process invoices and generate financial reports, making bookkeeping more efficient for entrepreneurs. There are various versions, depending on your needs, including desktop and cloud-based options.

Wave Accounting

Waveapps.com

Wave offers free accounting software for small businesses, including invoicing, expense tracking and financial reporting tools. The app is particularly popular with freelancers and very small businesses looking for an accessible way to manage their finances. It also offers paid services like payroll.

FreshBooks

Freshbooks.com

FreshBooks is cloud-based accounting software designed for small business owners and freelancers, particularly those in service-based industries. It simplifies financial management by offering tools for invoicing clients, tracking expenses and time, managing projects and generating financial reports.

MARKETING & WEB SOLUTIONS

Google My Business
business.google.com/us/business-profile/
Use this free tool to manage your online presence across Google, including both Search and Maps. It helps businesses appear in local search results, engage with customers through reviews and share important information like hours and contact details.

Canva
Canva.com
Canva is an online graphic design tool that helps entrepreneurs create professional-looking marketing materials without extensive design experience. It offers templates for social media posts, presentations, flyers, logos and more, making visual content creation accessible.

Mailchimp
Mailchimp.com
This all-in-one marketing platform helps small businesses manage email marketing campaigns, build landing pages, create websites and automate marketing efforts. It's a popular choice for building email lists and engaging with customers.

Squarespace
Squarespace.com
Another all-in-one platform, Squarespace helps companies build visually appealing websites, online stores and portfolios. It's known for its user-friendly interface and professionally designed templates, making it accessible for entrepreneurs to create a strong online

presence without needing extensive technical skills. It also offers features like scheduling, email campaigns and analytics.

Hootsuite

Hootsuite.com

This social media management platform helps you manage and schedule posts across multiple social networks from a single dashboard. I've used it before to streamline my social media efforts, support my content creation, schedule posts, track performance and manage customer engagement all in one place.

Hubspot

Hubspot.com

Hubspot provides an integrated suite of tools designed to help small businesses grow by managing their marketing, sales, customer service and content. It centralizes customer data, automates marketing campaigns, helps manage sales pipelines and provides tools for customer support, website building and analytics.

Constant Contact

Constantcontact.com

This email marketing and automation platform was made for small businesses and non-profits. It provides user-friendly tools for creating professional email campaigns, managing contact lists, segmenting audiences and tracking performance. It also offers features for building websites, e- commerce stores, social media marketing and event management.

MOTIVATIONAL BUSINESS PODCASTS

Startup (by Gimlet Media)

Gimletmedia.com/shows/startup

The Startup podcast offers a unique, unfiltered and often very personal look at what it's really like to start a business. The first season famously chronicled the launch of Gimlet Media itself, providing raw insights into the challenges, anxieties and small victories of entrepreneurship.

Subsequent seasons explore different startup stories, giving listeners a transparent view of the journey from idea to execution.

Masters of Scale

Mastersofscale.com

Hosted by LinkedIn co-founder Reid Hoffman, this podcast explores theories of how companies grow from zero to a global scale. Each episode features Hoffman testing his theories against the experiences of legendary leaders, providing deep insights into scaling strategies, leadership, innovation and company culture, often with a focus on tech and rapid growth.

The Smart Passive Income Online Business and Blogging Podcast

Smartpassiveincome.com

For anyone interested in building online businesses and creating multiple income streams, Pat Flynn's podcast is a comprehensive resource. He shares practical strategies, case studies and interviews with experts on topics like online business models, passive income, digital marketing and leveraging personal brands, all with an emphasis on transparency and actionable advice.

The $100 MBA Show
100mba.net

This daily podcast offers concise, actionable business lessons designed to teach entrepreneurs everything they need to know about starting and running a business without the fluff. Omar Zenhom breaks down complex business concepts into bite-sized, practical advice, covering a wide array of topics relevant to everyday entrepreneurial challenges and opportunities.

Recap: All Your Power Tips in One Place

Most of the chapters in this book ended with a list of four tips to get you started. Here they all are in one place for easy reference.

4 Ways to Crush Your Business Planning Game

- **Do the boring stuff first.** Figure out if anyone actually wants what you're selling and whether you can make money doing it before you dive in headfirst.

- **Use your plan as proof you've thought this through.** Show the world (and yourself) that you understand what you're getting into and have a reasonable plan for making it work.

- **Don't let excuses derail your planning.** You're going to invest months or years into this venture, so it's worth spending a weekend figuring out if you're headed in the right direction.

- **Get your ideas out of your head and onto paper.** Transform your organized chaos into a concrete roadmap that keeps your plan of action on track.

4 Quick Money Preservation Tips

- **Map your money:** Understand all initial investments & startup expenses.

- **Monitor cash flow:** Track your burn rate and identify revenue sources.

- **Establish boundaries:** Create separate business accounts (bank, credit, etc.).

- **Log every dollar:** Use simple tools to record all income and outgoing expenses.

4 Planning Hacks That Actually Work

- **Start with the essentials.** Focus on the seven core sections that matter and don't get bogged down trying to create a 50-page masterpiece that no one wants to read.

- **Remember the 260% advantage.** Entrepreneurs with business plans are 260% more likely to launch their companies, so you're literally improving your odds just by putting pen to paper.

- **Make it fit your business, not the template.** Your plan doesn't need to check every box in some generic framework, it needs to work for your specific situation and goals.

- **Think greatest hits, not encyclopedia.** Your executive summary should be like your business plan's greatest hits album, hitting the high notes in two pages or less.

4 Ways to Gain a Planning Edge

- **Start with what you know, guess where you don't.** You don't need perfect information to begin planning, just make your best educated guesses and fill in the blanks as you learn more about your business.

- **Think living document, not final exam.** Your business plan should grow and evolve with your understanding, so revisit and refine it regularly instead of treating it like a one-and-done assignment.

- **Skip what doesn't fit, but don't ignore the hard stuff.** Feel free to leave out sections that genuinely don't apply to your venture, but tackle the challenging parts because that's where the real value lies.

- **Use the samples when you're stuck.** Check out the completed examples in Chapters 4 and 5 of this book for inspiration and guidance when you hit a roadblock in your planning process.

References

This book grew out of years of reporting, research and lived experience, plus a business planning guide for REALTORS® that's been in print for about 20 years (and in its fourth edition) and still used by state associations to train their new agents.

While much of the content in this book comes from stories, insights and examples I've collected along the way, I also leaned on outside sources to fact-check, inspire and validate the advice you've read here. Here's a selection of key references and resources that supported the work, organized by chapter. All URLs were current and operational as of September 2025.

INTRODUCTION

Write Your Business Plan, U.S. Small Business Administration
sba.gov/business-guide/plan-your-business/write-your-business-plan

Hayes, Adam, Comprehensive Guide to Crafting a Winning Business Plan, Investopedia
investopedia.com/terms/b/business-plan.asp

How to Write a Business Plan, Step by Step, NerdWallet
nerdwallet.com/article/small-business/business-plan

CHAPTER 1

What Percentage of Small Businesses Fail? 2025 Data Reveals the Answer, Commerce Institute commerceinstitute.com/business-failure-rate

Small Business Statistics, Chamber of Commerce
chamberofcommerce.org/small-business-statistics

CHAPTER 2

Yaqub, M., 16+ Business Plan Statistics That You Must Know in 2024, BusinessDasher
businessdasher.com/business-plan-statistics

Frequently Asked Questions About Small Business, U.S. Small Business Administration
Advocacy.sba.gov

51 staggering small business statistics to know in 2024, CIN7
Cin7.com/blog/small-business-statistics

About the Author

First of all, much gratitude for allowing me to play a small role in your entrepreneurial journey. Know that I <u>do not</u> take that trust and responsibility lightly.

I'm Bridget McCrea. I've hustled through dead-end jobs, stretched a bank account that was almost empty, raised a toddler while chasing deadlines and built a business with nothing but determination, a desktop and a Texas Instruments 1200-baud modem at my kitchen table. For more than three decades I've been telling the real stories of entrepreneurs who took the same unpredictable path.

Three things I love most about being an entrepreneur & writer:

1. **Building something out of scraps.** I started with little more than grit, a toddler on my hip and a nearly empty bank account. I turned it into a business that lasted.

2. **Getting a front-row seat to other people's journeys.**
   From sitting across the table from inspiring female leaders like Mindy Grossman to hearing how R.W. Garcia's founders came up with the idea for tortilla salad strips, I've seen firsthand what it really takes to create something that lasts

3. **Turning lessons into tools that help others.**
   Whether it's writing seven books, crafting a Dummies guide for Wiley or developing content for well-known companies like Toyota, Panasonic and SAP, I love distilling hard-won insights into something others can actually use.

I've written for big-name media outlets, picked up a few awards along the way and published books that people still keep on their shelves. But the real win is seeing readers like you put the lessons to work. If *Blueprints Beat Cocktail Napkins* helps you take even one solid step toward building your business, then it's done its job.

Unlock Your Exclusive Business Planning Toolkit

As a thank you for buying *Blueprints Beat Cocktail Napkins*, here are four free bonus downloads to help you launch and grow with confidence. Think of this as your personal business planning toolkit, filled with practical guides, fillable worksheets and an easy-to-follow infographic you can start using right away.

Grab them anytime at www.bridgetmccrea.com/planningbonus or scan the QR code below.

- ⇨ **Your Business Plan Blueprint: An Interactive Planning Workbook (fillable PDF)**
  Developed specifically for entrepreneurs, this interactive business plan workbook will help you win more customers, close more deals & grow your profits.

- ⇨ **Sample Business Plan: Strategic Growth for Product Sales (PDF)**

- ⇨ **Sample Business Plan: Unlocking Growth Potential in the Service Sector (PDF)**

- ⇨ **6 Ways to Get the Biggest Bang for Your Planning Buck**
  Take these steps to maximize your business planning return on investment (ROI).

- ⇨ **10 Action Steps to Take to Kickstart Your New Business (infographic)**

Share Your Experience & Help Others Start Smart

Starting a business isn't easy and I know firsthand how overwhelming it can feel. If *Blueprints Beat Cocktail Napkins* helped you plan, launch or grow your business, would you take a minute to share that in an Amazon review?

Your words can encourage the next entrepreneur who's wondering whether they have what it takes. Reviews help others discover the book, see what's possible and take their first step.

Every review adds to a growing community of first-time business owners who are learning, building and succeeding together. I'd love for you to be part of it.

Made in the USA
Coppell, TX
13 January 2026

68244931R00066